W9-ABB-247

Advance Praise for

Are We There Yet

"In ARE WE THERE YET, Rabbi Shefa Gold reminds us that on the spiritual path, each step is the destination. Her spirituality infuses her travel with moments of being, just as her travel infuses her spirituality with movement and dynamism. This is a delightful little book.

— Rabbi Jay Michaelson, author of *The Gate of Tears: Sadness and the Spiritual Path*

"This is Rabbi Shefa at her quintessential, charismatic best: tour guide to life itself, demonstrating how every moment can open into discovery, awakening, revelation."

— Sylvia Boorstein, author of *That's Funny, You Don't Look Buddhist: On Being a Faithful Jew and a Passionate Buddhist*

"Go with Rabbi Shefa Gold on a powerful internal and external voyage. She will show you how to connect to nature, environment, God, and, ultimately, yourself. She takes you through pain and uncertainty to gratitude and awe. This is very intimate time with a spiritual leader who understands the true meaning of the word "spiritual." Be sure to read with a highlighter pen in hand because there are many gems you will want to go back to again and again."

—Judith Fein, author of *Life is a Trip* and *The Spoon from Minkowitz.*

"We are all nomads wandering in a world of physical, emotional, intellectual, and spiritual fluidity, and yet desperately grasping at anything that promises to maintain the illusion of constancy. With Shefa Gold as our guide, however, we transform desperation into inspiration, and wandering into wondering. ARE WE THERE YET is a travel guide for those who dare to walk not from here to there, but from here to here and here again."

—Rabbi Rami Shapiro, author of *The Tao of Solomon*

"Rabbi Shefa Gold takes us as happy companions on her globe-trotting adventures, and invites us into the inner journeys—hers and ours—that travel inspires. Pack your bags! In this picaresque book, you're in for an illuminating treat for your senses and a deep awakening of your soul."

—Rabbi Wayne Dosick, author *Living Judaism* and *The Real Name of God*

"In Are We There Yet, Rabbi Shefa Gold opens the door to her extraordinary life and treats us to her wise way of encountering the world. Full of spirited teachings, this book is a joy to read. Best of all, it invites us to wake up to our own journeys, and behold the magic all around us."

—Rabbi Tirzah Firestone, author of *With Roots In Heaven* and *Wounds Into Wisdom: Healing Intergenerational Jewish Trauma* (2019).

ARE WE THERE YET?

Travel as a Spiritual Practice

SHEFA GOLD

Ben Yehuda Press
Teaneck, New Jersey

http://www.BenYehudaPress.com

Ben Yehuda Press books may be purchased for educational, business or sales
promotional use. For information, please contact:
Special Markets, Ben Yehuda Press,
122 Ayers Court #1B, Teaneck, NJ 07666
markets@BenYehudaPress.com

ISBN13 978-1-934730-72-0

Library of Congress Cataloging-in-Publication Data

Names: Gold, Shefa, author.
Title: Are we there yet? : travel as a spiritual practice / Shefa Gold.
Description: Teaneck, New Jersey : Ben Yehuda Press, [2019] | Includes
    bibliographical references and index.
Identifiers: LCCN 2018047125 | ISBN 9781934730720 (pbk. : alk. paper)
Subjects: LCSH: Travel--Religious aspects--Judaism. | Travel etiquette. |
    Gold, Shefa--Travel. | Spiritual life--Judaism. | Jewish
    travelers--Anecdotes.
Classification: LCC BM720.T7 G65 2019 | DDC 296.7--dc23
LC record available at https://lccn.loc.gov/2018047125

21 20 19 / 10 9 8 7 6 5 4 3   20190104

Contents

Are We There Yet?

Imagine this scene: We see a tribe riding camels across the desert. The sun is burning; the wind is blowing; the wilderness stretches out before them. A boy riding on a camel next to his dad is whining, "Are we there yet?" The father calmly trudges on through the wilderness. In the next frame, the young boy repeats his question, and you get the feeling that he's been asking this same question all the long day. Finally, his father turns toward his son and in exasperation shouts, "For God's sake, we're **nomads**!"

To realize that we're nomads is to know the double truth that we're not there yet... and yet it is possible to know that we are always there, arriving wholly in this moment, fully present in this step, alive to the miracle of the journey.

We are *there* whenever we are awake.

Are We There Yet

The Gully:
My Training Ground for a Life of Travel

Back in the 1950s, when my parents came to northern New Jersey, they probably thought they were moving to the country. Our neighborhood was surrounded by farms and woods. As I grew up, just about all those farms and all those woods gave way to shopping malls and housing developments. By the time I was 8 or 9, there was just one precious plot of wild land left in Paramus right behind our back yard. We called it *The Gully*, and it was saved from development because it belonged to the Elks Club. This tiny scrap of wilderness was put to use for their annual picnic. The rest of the time it was my world, my place for adventure, exploration, clandestine pleasures and play. Well, not just mine: All the neighborhood kids played there. If you built a fort, some mean kid was sure to tear it down. Every tree, rock, or bush had a name. I had my hideouts, my secret places of refuge, portals to other worlds, places where my imagination could run wild.

The Gully was not without its dangers. I often came home scratched up and bleeding after fighting my way through blackberry bushes, or covered with the spreading itch of poison ivy. One time my brother and I were hopelessly stuck in mud (sure that it was quicksand), and once my boot came off in the snow and I limped home, numb with frostbite. I was serious about my play, and remember being indignant when my mom called me in for dinner. "But I'm playing!" I'd protest. Being an explorer was my job, my identity, my destiny.

The Gully was a microcosm of the whole wild world that awaited me, beyond the shopping malls, beyond the suffocation of school, outside the confines of suburban banalities. I refused to settle for ordinary. "I'm not from here," I insisted. "I'm from an island off the coast of Madagascar." (This was the most exotic place I could imagine.) By playing in the Gully, I developed a taste for adventure; I had a glimpse of the endless expanse that was hidden in plain sight.

The Gully was the outer scene for my inner explorations. I remember being fascinated by the phenomenon of déja vu. I would make up elaborate explanations that involved other dimensions and parallel universes. I devised intricate and elegant stories that gave me reasons to be both fascinated and terrified.

"If you fell into the crack between moments you might tumble into eternity and never come back!" And in spite of my terror, how I yearned to fall!

"I knew that at the moment of my birth, another soul was also born on the other side of the world, who was also **me**. *How we yearned to be reunited! And yet if we were ever to meet face-to-face, the whole universe as we know it would be destroyed!"*

In the Gully I explored these yearnings and these terrors, while nibbling sweet peas, blackberries and wild scallions. My adventures in the Gully prepared me for a life of travel. This tiny patch of land, bordered by backyards, a cement factory, a highway and The Elks Club was my training ground. The roar of trucks on Route 17 was the roar of the world, calling me.

It felt like the most natural thing in the world to claim the whole wide world as my own, to exult in mobility and follow my impulse toward new horizons.

I designed a life for myself that would allow me to travel and see the whole world as my teacher and friend. And I wanted a life where I could be continually challenged, so that each new challenge might send me to call on the resources that were buried inside me.

Often, my friends or acquaintances see my travel schedule and then turn to me with a look of pity. They say, "Oh it must be so hard," or, "When are you going to stop traveling so much? It must be terrible to be on the road like that."

And I say, "Traveling is my practice."

I wrote this book to explain what it means to make traveling a practice, to learn from the road and surrender to each step of the journey, and then make that step my home.

I meet so many people on the road who seem only to want to get where they're going. "Are we there yet?" Well, yes. And, no.

Yes. The spiritual practice of travel teaches me how to be *there* in every step, to fully inhabit the multi-dimensional experience of this moment. Through travel, I am learning how to show up and make myself fully available and receptive to the gift that God (the Great Mystery) is giving me just *now*.

And, no, I will never get *there* because the destination is a dynamic force calling me onward with the roar of the world, opening me up, sending me always toward my ever-expanding potential.

The Path of Pilgrimage

In 1980 I hitchhiked through Europe with a guitar, a change of clothes, a tent and a sleeping bag. I was learning the *Art of the Road*. I was learning to open my eyes. I traveled without a set itinerary, determined to open myself to a new adventure each day. Daily, I was forced to let go of expectations, and I encountered generosity in the most unexpected places. I kept making plans, only to see them dissolve in the light of startling synchronicities and unforeseen encounters. Every place of rigidity in me was forced to bend or soften.

As I stood at the tip of the Greek mainland, at the Temple of Poseidon, I heard the call of Jerusalem. I decided to make my journey into a pilgrimage. I imagined standing before the Western Wall of the ancient Temple and bringing the force of my whole life's longing as my offering to lay before God. I imagined standing before that Wall with so much love that all the walls between myself and God might be shattered.

In that moment of *Intention*, my journey was transformed. At one level I still looked like a sightseer, entertained by history and strange customs. Yet I also knew that as a pilgrim, each step of my journey had the power to strip me bare, so that I might finally stand before God and know myself.

It was a wonderful and dangerous journey. The military had recently taken over the government in Turkey; there was a civil war going on in Syria; and then the Iran/Iraq

War broke out, with Syria and Jordan taking sides against each other. I was learning about the subtle arts of survival, bargaining and bribery. I was, for the first time, stepping out of the Western world-view, learning new rules and un-learning so much that I had believed certain.

Meanwhile, I was keeping a meticulous journal of my inner life. I knew that each strange scene I confronted was reflecting back to me some aspect of my inner landscape that I had till that day been ignoring. I was determined to use each step of my pilgrimage as a vehicle for self-discovery. I was determined to see each person I met as a messenger who had come to teach me something essential.

I arrived at the Wall in Jerusalem in the middle of the night in the pouring rain. I was tired but more alive than I had ever been. Each outward step toward Jerusalem had also been an inward step of uncovering the complexities of my own heart. The daily Jewish prayer says, *LiYerushalay-im ircha, b'rachamim tashuv.* To Jerusalem Your City, you will return with Compassion.

As I approached that ancient holy wall, I tried to keep my heart steady with compassion. The sound of rain against stone seemed like the tears of all my ancestors flooding me now... and then I heard a voice, calling me. "Hey Baby, come here and kiss me!" I could not believe it. The voice was coming from the guard booth at the edge of the courtyard where a bored but insistent Israeli soldier was beckoning to me.

I turned to him, exasperated. I sighed and thought, "I can't believe you're ruining this historic moment!"

Turning back toward the Wall, I tried to compose myself and focus my intention to be wholehearted before God. The whole time I stood there praying, the soldier kept yelling through the rain, "Kiss me, Kiss me!" And I couldn't help but laugh.

Many years later I studied the Song of Solomon whose opening line says, "Kiss me with the kisses of your mouth, for your sweet loving is better than wine."

Finally, I am able to receive the hidden message of my pilgrimage. That obnoxious Israeli guard who only knew a few words of English was my messenger, my angel, come to tell me:

God is calling you to intimacy with the Reality before you. "Kiss me," Life says. "Open to the truth of God in this moment. Open to the fullness of pleasure and pain. Every time you turn toward the past or toward an abstract idea, I will call you back to Me through a simple yet profound engagement with Life. Your sweet loving is better than wine, better than an abstract ideal, better than getting high, better than fame, better than sex, better than knowing a lot, better than success. Kiss me, Kiss me!"

To embark on a pilgrimage is to be open to the message that you have spent your whole life resisting. To embark on a pilgrimage is to be willing to leave behind the familiar comforts, habits, addictions and self-definitions, and walk straight into the Truth of who you were meant to be.

When I travel, I am learning to be a pilgrim rather than a tourist. A tourist goes someplace in order to get something: a beautiful view, an interesting experience, perhaps some souvenirs to bring home.

When I can transform my journey into a pilgrimage, then with each step I am opening to the blessing of *this* place; and with each step I am bringing blessing to *this* place. The giving and receiving of blessing gives me a purpose that changes the quality of my presence. As a pilgrim I lose my interest in shopping, and it even feels a bit awkward to take pictures. As a pilgrim, I am allowing myself to be moved. I am honoring this place as the doorway between this finite world and the infinite mystery. I am honoring this moment as the culmination of all the moments I have lived thus far. I am also honoring all the beings who have trod this ground beneath my feet as I receive the accumulated bounty of their devotion and experience.

A pilgrimage begins the moment I realize that I need this, and I resolve to go. I need a pilgrimage when I have stopped *seeing* the world before me. I need a pilgrimage when my world has shrunk too small, or my habits have overshadowed my spontaneity. I need a pilgrimage when I realize that a chapter of my life has ended, yet the new chapter remains shrouded. I need to step out of the flow and momentum of my life in order to get some perspective on the whole journey.

A pilgrimage requires me to bring an offering, and then open wide to receive a gift of that place. A pilgrimage requires me to receive that gift on behalf of my family, friends, communities and kindred souls... and then to bring it back to them.

I was once invited to a celebration of a Bedouin tribe at the edge of the ancient city of Petra, in Jordan. It was there that I learned the meaning of pilgrimage. They slaughtered a goat and roasted it over a fire at dusk. The whole tribe gathered. They were clearly overflowing with joy and generosity. One of their tribe had taken a pilgrimage, a long and dangerous journey to a far-off shrine, and he had come home safely. What I understood from this celebration was that everyone in the tribe had been honored and blessed by the success of this one man's journey. He had journeyed on their behalf, and the whole community knew themselves to be raised up in stature in the eyes of God.

Though I politely declined to partake of the goat, I did devour the joy and was sated with celebration. I danced with the Bedouins and shared in their grateful celebration. By the end of the night we were covered with dust kicked up in the dance and ashes that wafted out from the fire. The pilgrim rested in the embrace of his community, and they had been honored by the gift of his return.

This set me to wondering, "Who would celebrate my return? How might I travel on behalf of others? What could I bring back from my journeys that would benefit my beloveds back home?"

Just asking these questions changes the way I travel.

Driving

I love to move. Walking, skipping, jumping, swimming, flying—they all point me toward freedom. Every kind of movement helps me come unstuck, and reminds me that I am part of a larger dance. Gabriel Roth, the great teacher of Ecstatic Practice, challenges us, asking, "If *you* don't do your dance, who will?"

Sometimes I call God the *Great Choreographer*. I am taking direction, listening for the call to move that sings from deep within my heart and body wisdom.

All of those impulses toward movement send me to a deeper stillness. And then in that stillness, I can hear even more clearly the subtle messages of the Great Choreographer.

In the Book of Genesis, our ancestor, Abram (later his name became Abraham) hears a call to step forth into the dance of his destiny. "Get going," God tells him. "Leave the land of your birth and family. Leave everything that you know and step into the unknown place that I will show you. Then I will bless you and you will become a blessing."

As a teenager in suburban New Jersey, I heard this same call to "get going." Somehow, I knew that to fulfill this Divine command, I would need a car. The only way for me to "do my dance" was to get out of my parents' house.

For me, a car meant freedom, independence, mobility, self-determination and autonomy. While my Bat Mitzvah might have been the beginning of claiming my identity, getting a car was truly my rite of passage into adulthood.

I got a job in a candle factory and worked full time after school, from 4:00 pm till midnight, coming home each night smelling like one of those scented candles—cinnamon, jasmine, lemon, pine or rose. I worked the wicking machine, listening carefully to all its clicks and whirring. I learned how to fix the machine when it broke down, because I knew every part of its song.

Finally, I earned enough money to buy a used, slightly beat-up Plymouth station wagon with a push-button transmission. To my eyes, she was beautiful.

I learned to drive from my older brother, Harold, who was unflappable. He met my nervousness with calm, my high drama with cool reasonableness. He made driving look easy. His easy-going nature was contagious. I set out to learn the lessons of the road.

To drive safely I needed to learn two important skills, and those skills have served me everywhere, both on and off the road.

The first skill was learning to drive with the awareness that there is a blind spot; you must accept that there is something that you do not yet see. When you know about the blind spot, you drive (and live) differently; you're always a bit doubtful of your own limited perspective. You learn to be both relaxed and alert.

Now that's how I always want to be. Being relaxed means continually letting go of tension and worry. When I'm in a state of constriction, I can't receive the blessing that God is trying to give me, and it's a state that I can't sustain without doing damage to myself or others. Being alert means that I am continually moving in the direction of more awareness. I'm awake and continually awakening to the depth and scope of this life's adventure.

Knowing that I have a blind spot keeps me humble, keeps me seeking and learning.

The second skill I learned from driving, but apply to the whole of my life, is this: You must maintain a dual attention. Even as you focus on the road ahead of you, you establish a wider field of awareness. The low beams keep you focused and the high beams open your perspective to the bigger picture. You keep your eyes on the road, but you're also scanning the periphery, noticing a stray dog that might dart into the highway, seeing that motorcycle out of the corner of your eye, watching for anomalies in the pattern of traffic flow.

This skill of dual attention is so very useful as a traveler. I can be completely focused on this moment, present in this step, enjoying it with my whole being—and yet I am also taking in, and being blown away by, the whole adventure of my life in all its vast dimensions and depths. In fact, it is my perception of the whole that sends me to a state of exquisite presence as I navigate each small step on the journey. And when I can really focus my attention on this step in all its miraculous detail, then I am gifted with a sense of my whole journey unfolding as part of the *Divine Choreography*.

With my newly acquired driving skills, I was ready for the next adventure. My Argentine artist boyfriend and I found an attic apartment in a house just ten miles away, in a wooded neighborhood that bordered on farmland. We set the date for moving and started packing.

My mother was adamantly opposed to my plan. The prescribed pathway for leaving home was going to college, living in a dorm, then getting married, finding a job, buying a house, and having kids. That was totally *not* my plan, not my path. She threatened to disown me. My poor distraught mother begged, cajoled, and pulled out all her best guilt-inducing ammunition … to no avail.

I remember that cool Spring day so clearly and my mother's last words to me echoing through the house as she left for work. "I forbid you to do this."

After packing my car, I sat for a moment in front of my childhood home, savoring the elixir of courage and joy that flooded my body. Then I turned the key, and pushed the button marked D for DRIVE.

The Sense of Danger

A Sense of Danger opens the way to aliveness, surprise and awareness, rather than fear, complacency and timidity. I don't mean the adrenaline kind of danger. I don't mean taking unnecessary risks. For the traveler, every step is a risk. And I take that step from the known into the unknown as a way of cultivating a heightened awareness of how precious, how fragile, and how significant is this very moment. A sense of danger can become the inspiration for honing intuition and paying exquisite attention.

As a young teenager, I would take the bus from New Jersey into New York City on weekends, just to wander around. I'd get lost and then try to find my way back. I remember following a man who was whistling and then finding myself somewhere unfamiliar, somewhere I never would have found, feeling that I had been led there for a reason. Many of those city streets were not safe. This was during the time of the heroin epidemic in New York. So I learned to follow the voices within that warned, "No, not this one. Take the next block." Because I was interested, curious, and not in a hurry, I seemed to be a magnet for what I called "crazy people." But I also listened to the voice inside me that said, "Better to avoid this one." My keen sense of danger allowed me to expand my perspectives beyond my white, middle-class roots, and beyond ideas of what was deemed "normal."

I witnessed a lot of suffering, had some close calls, made stupid mistakes—but through it all I kept on learning. I learned to keep one pocket of change just for panhandlers. As soon as I put that money in my pocket, I knew that it was no longer mine. It belonged to those people on the street.

I enjoyed having nowhere to go, which meant I could end up anywhere.

One of the great lessons of travel is: Don't get too attached to your plan, and leave some time for wandering.

When I was 19, my Argentine artist boyfriend and I were invited by a renowned sculptor to live and work in an artist colony is southern France. It was such an honor to be included in a community of artists. We thought that it was a dream come true! I would compose music and he would paint. It was such a good plan. But when we arrived there, the dream went sour. We didn't feel welcome; people weren't friendly at all; neither of us knew a word of French. So, after about three days we left and found our way to Ibiza, an island off the coast of Spain. There we squatted in a stone hut on the grounds of an abandoned orchard, and were joined by adventurers from all over the world. We shared our humble quarters with a Mexican prince and Marcel Marceau's son.

I learned that by giving up my plan I became vulnerable. That vulnerability forced me to connect with others. A sense of danger accompanied me on my journey—the danger of not knowing what would happen next. In surrendering to that state of not-knowing, every encounter became a meaningful, surprising and magical teaching.

I learned that if you *play it safe*, you'll miss out on the surprise. Sometimes you just have to leap.

The more I cultivate a sense of safety inside me, the easier it is to face the necessary risks of travel and the dangers that are inherent in a life of ever-expanding, ever-deepening adventure. The leap I am able to take depends on the degree of firmness of the rock on which I stand. For me, that rock is my basic trust in Reality, a deep knowing that I am held, and that I am ultimately going to be okay, no matter what. "Even Death is safe," my soul whispers.

The more I can cultivate that sense of being held, the more I can let go of tension and rigidity, and just relax into the expanded moment of what is. The more I can relax, the more I can enjoy and receive the unique gift of this moment. If I walk around feeling that I am the one holding my world together, then all my effort goes into that holding. When I relax and lean back into the Divine Embrace, then all that energy I was using to just hold on tight can be redirected into my creative life.

And so, the practice that supports and sustains me in travel is to cultivate and nurture my basic trust. One way to do this is by *planting glimpses*. We all have moments of knowing, moments of remembering that we are perfectly connected, inextricably bound to all of Creation. In that small moment, all is right with the world; we are given a glimpse of perfection.

And then that moment fades. We fall back into the so-called *real world* of struggle and harsh dualities.

But I have found that if I can bring awareness to the very moment of knowing and deep connection—the moment when the boundaries of self and world dissolve—I can use that awareness to plant that glimpse like a seed. Every time I touch that feeling of connection and *Oneness*, I am nurturing that seed, growing my sense of basic trust in the universe that holds me.

Then, when it comes time to let go of my plan, step out of my outgrown identity and step into a new and wilder possibility, I have the firmness under my feet that will allow me to leap.

Finding Laughter

Nearly a year after the breakup of my marriage, I was just beginning to feel alive again, glimmers of hope peeking out from the shadows of despair that had fallen over my heart. I was teaching in Holland and I had a free week between workshops, during which time I had hoped to play and perhaps free my broken heart from some of its burden. It was a cold and rainy July and the weather perfectly mirrored my dark mood. As I walked the streets of Amsterdam a glossy picture of a sunny beach in Greece caught my eye. I stepped into the office of a travel agency and said, "Please, get me out of here!"

Well, it just so happened that there was a special week-long excursion leaving the next day for the island of Corfu, which included airfare and lodging at an amazingly affordable price.

I joined a group of Dutch tourists who were all avid, ardent soccer fans. None of them spoke English, and even if they had, would only have wanted to talk about the World Cup. We were taken to a remote hotel on the northeastern coast of Corfu, a stone's throw from the forbidding coast of Albania. Surrounded by Dutch soccer fans, my sense of aloneness was magnified; so I retreated to my room, which had a balcony that spilled out onto the rocky beach. For three days I sat and watched the waves tumble over white, sun-bleached stones. I wrote in my journal while I let the rhythmic sea, astonishingly blue sky, gentle breeze and bright sun heal me. I let myself rest and feel held. I let the turmoil of my heart settle into calm. By the third day, I felt a lot better. That morning I wrote in my journal, "I'm beginning to feel grateful again for my life. But there's just one thing. I haven't found my laughter." I remembered what it felt like to laugh, and I longed to feel that humor and lightness of spirit again.

That day I decided to take the bus into the nearest village to have lunch. The only restaurant was crowded with both locals and tourists, so I waited on line. The only other English speakers in the crowd waited with me, and when a table became available we agreed to share it.

While we waited for our lunch, the young man introduced himself as a pastor in a church in the north of England. Well, of course I told him that I was a rabbi, and we fell into an animated conversation about our ministries. He said, "Mine is a laughing church." He explained that one day, the Spirit just captured the entire congregation and sent them all into uncontrollable laughter. Some people laughed so hard they fell on the floor and had to be carried out to their cars at the end of the service. Apparently, this was a phenomenon that was spreading across the world. No one really understood it, but it was received as a great blessing and was revitalizing his church.

When our food came, the three of us held hands, and then both the pastor and his wife prayed for me, that I might receive the gift of Laughter.

My laughter did gradually return, and now I know it as an essential part of who I am. And yes, there are messengers everywhere. They will find me when I am ready.

Burnt Bagel Breakthrough

Walking up 7th Avenue in New York City on a sunny winter morning, pulling my suitcase toward Port Authority Bus Station, my mood was expansive, and I was feeling grateful for the leisure that would allow me to choose the quintessential New York breakfast place. I saw a sign that shouted, "Breakfast Special $3.45. 2 eggs, toast and home fries," and I knew this was *the place*.

I schlepped my suitcase to a back table and then waited on line at the cafeteria-style counter while I watched a sweet, diligent, extended family of workers who I imagined were Guatemalan farmers transplanted to the city. They were flipping eggs and juggling plates in perfect communication with each other. Their wide-open faces concentrated on the task of feeding hundreds of busy tourists, office workers, and shopkeepers on their way to work.

The young man behind the counter offered me a smile as he handed me my breakfast special. I had asked for a bagel and was looking forward to a real New York bagel. Living in New Mexico I never could trust the bagels of the Southwest. What do they know from bagels?

Well, the eggs were fine, the home fries plenty, but the bagel was burnt! I hesitated for just a second and then carried my tray back to the table. A little background here: I've always hated burnt toast. I always order carefully at restaurants. "Lightly toasted please," I demand as clearly and as nicely as I can.

But this time, holding this burnt bagel, my whole life of

wanting what I want, asking for what I want and getting what I want comes into question. The *me* that likes some things and hates other things suddenly recedes—and I am quite simply grateful for the breakfast special that God, the Universe, the Guatemalan family has made for me. I bless and eat this blackened bagel. I am fully present to receive its unique taste and texture. Suddenly there is no judgment. All of my preferences are gone. It tastes exactly like a burnt bagel, but my whole story about what I like and how I like it is gone. With every bite, I think, "This is so interesting." I feel so light.

And I know that I have tasted Freedom.

There is a part of me that is always seeking pleasure and comfort, while trying to avoid pain and relieve discomfort. And from this urge toward pleasure and away from pain, I can build up a fixed set of preferences that are rarely questioned or challenged. With my preferences, I build a world that I imagine to be safe.

When I travel, I notice that part of me that is looking for the familiar and seeking comfort. It's amazing how my brain registers that Starbucks green goddess symbol far down at the end of the concourse, and a smile inches across my face in anticipation of that familiar comfort before I even realize what's happening. Or I become positively giddy with anticipation of a hot shower as I emerge from a wilderness journey.

I also notice that when I can step outside my comfort zone, I am often rewarded with an experience of surprising depth and transformative realization. My sense of entitlement (*I deserve this; I paid for it; life should be what I want it to be*) is often the main obstacle to gratefulness for this moment exactly as it is. Gratefulness is a quality that connects me with the Source, allowing me to relax and receive the gift that I am being given just now. In Gratefulness, I am filled with energy, inspiration and generosity.

I don't expect I'll ever lose my preferences. I still like my bagels lightly toasted. But when I travel, I learn again and again that it's my attachments to those preferences that will make my journey complicated and difficult.

In my constant argument with Reality (what *is*)—Reality always seems to win.

Flight

As a young child I had an imaginary friend who took me on journeys throughout the universe and instilled in me my love of daydreaming. By the time I started school, I had lost touch with him. What remained was a suspicion that there was a secret world that just might be more real than the reality I was being shown. As that suspicion grew, my inner world expanded.

As a teenager I became increasingly unhappy with school. Feeling bored, misunderstood and angry, I began to daydream deliberately as a way to manage my despair. I would close my eyes, and call out to my old spirit-friend, Flight, and he would take me on a magical journey, away from my misery. It was the perfect escape. Or so I thought.

One day in Biology class, I closed my eyes, and Flight whisked me away. When I returned, I was left shaken and terrified. You see, I hadn't invited Flight to come. I suddenly felt vulnerable, out of control and terrified, as if I might be teetering on the edge of madness. I realized that staying in school, being in a place where I didn't want to be, was dangerous to my sanity.

Determined to save myself, I quit high school, and together with 12 other kids from around the county, started a Free School. In our school we decided what to learn and how to learn. We found teachers, became teachers to each other, and then began seeing the whole world as our classroom. Free School saved my life and set me on a path of self-realization, curiosity, inquiry and self-responsibility.

From that first day of Free School, I vowed to love my world, and rise to its challenges. And Flight, my wondrous companion, just vanished. In fact, I completely forgot all about him—for about 35 years.

I was at a conference for rabbis in Boulder, Colorado, at a special session for students of Ellen Kaufman Dosick, a great healer and visionary. Ellen has the ability to tune into subtle levels of energy and presence. She is both open and articulate. As our session began, Ellen seemed to have a moment of fluster. She began with an exclamation, "Flight is here!" And then she said, "Well I don't know what that means... " Everyone giggled, shifted in their seats and then we continued with the session.

But when I heard the name *Flight*, I was suddenly flooded with a whole series of vivid memories. All of those amazing adventures and the one traumatic journey that slammed one door shut while opening another door to my new life.

I asked Ellen to meet with me privately that evening in the hotel bar.

We secluded ourselves in a corner table, ordered drinks, and let the clatter of glasses and the clamor of conversation fade into the background as Ellen tuned in to my questions. She called in the being that I knew as Flight and allowed us to have a tearful reunion. He expressed deep remorse at having scared me that day in my 11th grade biology class. I gave him my fullest forgiveness and then felt my own remorse that I had cut him off so abruptly and had shut down the channel of love between us. Flight reminded me of the many years of adventure through my childhood that we were privileged to share. This reunion was a profound healing.

And then Ellen asked, "What kind of being are you?"

Ellen sat quietly and listened. Then she turned to me and said, "Flight tells me that he is an Awakener—and so are you."

What does it mean to be an *Awakener*? And how can all our journeys be voyages of awakening? The only way to be an Awakener would be to be awake myself. Only then could the quality of my presence have an influence in this world.

My experiences with Flight showed me that Reality is so much bigger than I could ever imagine. As we enter into the routines of life, our sense of the world tends to shrink. Sometimes, my world shrinks to exactly the size of my to-do list, because that's where my focus turns to each day. And sometimes, I am just living on autopilot, just trying to get things done, just trying to keep afloat, just trying to pay the bills, just treading water, just trying to stay out of trouble, just trying to avoid too much conflict.

Sometimes, I'm just trying to get comfortable or maintain a sense of security for myself and my loved ones. In search of safety, my tendency is to contract, and make my world smaller. Yet this contraction comes with a steep price. My heart closes. My body gets tense and rigid; my breath becomes short and shallow.

With all that energy and effort, all that I have built are my own defenses, and the illusion of safety.

My adventures with Flight opened up possibilities that were as wide as my imagination. We are all in the process of awakening to these possibilities. To be fully conscious and awake means to have the energy, love, and awareness to make the best choice in each moment, and to find joy inside us in both good times and bad. Flight showed me that joy.

Four Hour Layover

When I book a flight, I like to have a connection of about an hour. With an hour's leeway, I won't stress if my flight is just a few minutes late. I have enough time to find my connection, get a snack and use the facilities.

In booking a trip to the East Coast, there weren't many good choices and I ended up with a four-hour layover at Midway in Chicago, a smallish and not very interesting airport. It took less than an hour to explore the place and find something good to eat. Bored and restless, I sat and wondered how best to use my time. I heard an announcement about a prayer service in the airport chapel. "All are welcome," it said.

I took that as an invitation. To get to the chapel, you had to go down an empty hallway and get on an elevator that led to the administrative offices. It was like being backstage, and the airport personnel stared at me as if I was quite possibly an intruder.

I waited in the empty chapel, which was just another office, though festooned with crosses. When the service was about to begin, a large bear-like robed evangelical minister with an open and expressive face introduced himself to me with his booming preacher voice. It was just me. And Bill. I was his congregation, just one lone rabbi on her way to somewhere. We chatted for a moment and then he said, "Should I do my thing?"

I gave him an enthusiastic "Yes!" and he performed a beautiful service filled with scripture, prayer and exclamations of love. Being there with Bill made me forget where I was. He asked me what I needed (which was to learn how to keep my heart open) and then he prayed for me. I asked about his needs in turn, and Bill's voice suddenly softened. He launched into a long story about how he was caring for a disabled wife who was also suffering from dementia. I prayed for him with all my heart. We embraced in that holy space and then I was on my way, stepping back into the buzz of a busy airport.

It was the same dull airport, but now everything looked different. Everyone I passed looked mysterious or funny or interesting or eccentric. I was smiling with my whole face, walking with a spring in my step, filled with enthusiasm for the journey. And then I stopped in utter surprise as I saw a familiar face coming toward me.

Just a couple days before my trip, I had been thinking about Rose, who had been a student in my training. I hadn't seen Rose in many years, but she was on my mind. I had no idea why. It was just a feeling that there was something unfinished. I was feeling some remorse and confusion, and I was wondering what had kept me from connecting with her. I was searching my own heart, wondering if I should reach out to her, but I didn't know what I would say.

And there she was, walking toward me.

We hugged, and I spilled my tea. Rose blessed me by saying, "May that be the worst thing that ever happens to you in your travels." We made a short sweet connection before boarding our separate planes.

Taking off into the darkening skies on my way to Hartford,

I looked down at my tea-stained dress and felt truly blessed.

The longest journey we take is from that state of boredom, distraction, restlessness and disappointment to the place of gratefulness, expectancy, surprise and curiosity. That journey is not merely long: It's tricky. Why? Because when we are in that negative state, we are lost. We quite literally don't know where we are.

I thought I was in a boring airport (without even a Starbucks!) but truly I was in a place of miracle, where prayer could open my heart, where startling synchronicities could send me to clear old blockages, where blessing could flow.

Sitting there in Midway Airport, I wasn't completely lost because I could still hear the call, that announcement to come to the chapel. I could still feel invited. The Song of Songs has a beautiful line that says, "I was asleep, but my heart was awake." Truly that's a description of where I live a good deal of the time. It's not even my whole heart that is awake... just a small corner of my heart, just a glimmer of light, a spark of awareness. But that spark is enough to send me on a journey.

My faith is that if I take that journey often enough from the dull tedium of world-weariness to the sparkling clarity and shining mystery of knowing I am exactly in the right place at the right time, then I'll finally realize that this sparkling, shining mystery is my *home*.

Open to the Miracle of Happenstance

I was 45 minutes early to meet my old friend Nash at her office at 26th Street and 7th Avenue in New York City, so I took the opportunity to sit by the window of a teashop on the corner to observe the bustle of New York City pass by and do some seriously playful people-watching. What I've always loved about New York City is the feeling of sitting still and letting the whole world come to me. I found my stillness with a cup of tea and a ginger pastry and a perfect view of the busy sidewalk. A few minutes into my reverie, I spotted an older woman, kind of harried, kind of disheveled, and she happened to look right at me as I looked at her—so I waved. She seemed startled and didn't wave back. But she turned the corner and entered the teashop, came right up to me, and demanded, "Do I know you?"

When I said no, she asked, "Then, why did you wave to me?"

"Just being friendly," I replied.

She was flustered at first. This was not New York City behavior and she looked at me suspiciously. Then the woman softened and said, "Are you Jewish?"

"Not only am I Jewish," I answered, "I'm a rabbi!"

Well, this stopped her in her tracks, and she began telling me an amazing story. She said, "Do you know who Reb Nachman is?" I nodded. (Reb Nachman is a rabbi born in 1772 in the Ukraine.) "Well," she continued, "I talk to him all the time. You see, I've been having some problems, and I heard about a rabbi in Brooklyn who might be able to help me, so just yesterday, I asked Reb Nachman for permission to go see this rabbi in Brooklyn. And he said, 'No, you must find a *woman* rabbi.' And I told him 'I don't know how to find a woman rabbi.'"

She sat down and asked for my name. When I told her, she said, "I know about Shefa Gold!" She repeated my name out loud a few times. She was just incredulous, and excited that her disembodied rebbe had sent me to her. It turns out that she had been to a couple of congregations that use my music in their services. We both basked in the synergy, and then I did a short spiritual direction session with her right then and there. We talked about her problem. I don't know whether anything I said was helpful, but I do know that both of us walked away glowing and awed by the miracle of happenstance.

My journey is shaped by a simple, two-word prayer, which I don't always have the strength, presence or discernment to say. But on some days, I wake up and I feel ready to open and surrender to the flow of life.

On those days I simply turn to God, The Great Mystery, and say, "*Use me.*"

And then I just watch for opportunities to be of service. I pay careful attention to the impulse of my heart to be helpful, to show up—even if it's only with a smile or a wave or a door held open.

There is a great longing in me to be useful, to feel myself sent on a mission that matters. I know for sure that my very small gesture is just a tiny contribution, yet that gesture connects me somehow to a vast web of goodness. When I say, "*Use me*," I don't know how I'll be deployed. The mystery of it requires me to follow my intuition, step out of my complacency, and surrender to some larger work. There's a Johnny Appleseed quality to this aspect of the journey. I am planting seeds everywhere, with great faith. all the while detached from the results of my planting.

The Moshiach is Coming ...
Well, Maybe Not Yet

My journey began with an invitation from the Dean of Students at the Jewish Theological Seminary (JTS) to teach a workshop and lead a prayer service for the students there. For over 130 years, JTS has served as the intellectual and spiritual center of the Conservative Movement.

I grew up at a Conservative Temple at a time when women were not encouraged to be leaders. As a young girl I loved going to *Shul* with my Dad; I loved the prayers and the singing and the flowers and brownies at the *oneg* (reception afterwards). Both boys and girls were welcome to come up to the *bima* to open the *ark* or hold the candle, wine or spices for *Havdalah*. But as adolescence rolled around, girls were demoted. We were no longer welcome on the bima; we weren't allowed to read from the Torah.

Now that I was older, my questions weren't considered cute anymore. They were met with irritation.

I know now that my rabbis did me a great favor by excluding me, because I was the kind of person who thrives in an atmosphere of opposition. Just tell me what I can't do, and the spark will be planted, the yearning will be ignited, the fires will be fanned.

I left the synagogue on a long roundabout journey as a seeker of God, an explorer of the Mysteries. My journey took me far and wide through many spiritual traditions and practices, eventually spiraling back to Judaism. I became a lover of Torah, of the sacred texts of my heritage, and an innovator of how those texts might become relevant, useful and vital for me. For many years I was vilified and mocked by the guardians of Jewish institutions and traditions. I accepted that role in stride, feeling on the one hand hurt and misunderstood, and on the other hand affirmed as a would-be prophet. I remained ever hopeful.

So when the invitation came to teach at JTS, I laughed in delight and blurted out to my friends, "The Moshiach (Messiah) is surely coming!" It's an old joke that Jews say when something remarkable—something that we thought might never happen—is actually going to happen.

When I have an invitation to teach, I'm always careful to leave lots of time for travel, just in case there's a mishap along the way. I didn't calculate for three storms and a bus accident!

I live a half mile up a steep mesa, so I left the car at the bottom of my hill just in case it snowed in the mountains overnight. And of course, it did. I hitched a ride down to my car on the garbage truck the next morning, suitcase in tow. The road to the airport was fine and my flights were scheduled to leave on time. My first flight to Chicago went off without a hitch. And then the winds picked up and snow started to come down thick and constant. My flight to LaGuardia was delayed, delayed again, and then cancelled. I was rebooked on a flight in the morning, and I thought, "I can still make it. My workshop's not till late afternoon." I imagined that God was testing me, throwing obstacles in my path. My faith remained strong. My delight would not flicker. My determination would not waver. My resolve was strong and clear.

After a few hours of sleep, I boarded a flight for New York early the next morning, and the skies were clear. An hour into the flight, another storm, this one completely unexpected, filled the sky. We were rerouted to Norfolk, Virginia. As we sat on the tarmac, my fellow passengers and I looked at each other, incredulous, saying, "Where are we?" And I was thinking about Jonah and the sailors, wondering if I should just get off here. But of course, we were not allowed to deplane.

After a couple hours we left for New York, and the snow had turned to ice. I was beginning to sense the epic, mythic nature of this journey, but I was still laughing, and still determined. I picked up my luggage and boarded a bus heading toward Manhattan, my Promised Land.

The Grand Central Parkway was a sheet of ice, and our bus driver had nerves of steel. The highway was littered with cars that had skidded out of control. And then, inevitably, it was our turn. Though our heroic driver was calmly steering into each skid, somehow avoiding every obstacle, we swerved and found ourselves in a dizzying spin crossing multiple lanes, finally coming to a stop, facing the wrong way. It seemed no one was breathing. The driver jumped up to see if everyone had survived and we all took a breath realizing that we were indeed still alive, though shaken. He calmly turned the bus around and somehow made it to the Port Authority Bus Terminal where we were deposited into the icy slush. I gave that driver a hug and slipped him a twenty when he handed me my baggage.

Though happy to be alive, I realized that the entire city was shut down. There would be no workshop at JTS.

Three times in the Song of Songs, one of the central mystical texts of Judaism, it says, "Do not awaken Love until it is ripe." In other words, "Timing is everything." There had been one small window of possibility and now that window was closed, slammed shut, and locked against the storm.

If my invitation to JTS had been a sign that Moshiach was coming, in the wake of my epic journey interrupted by three storms and a bus accident, I reconsidered… well, maybe not yet.

Matthew Fox tells a story about what happened in Christian Europe as the year 1000 was approaching. People were sure that this was the end of days, that the messiah would be coming and bringing with him an era of peace, love and justice. And so, months before that expected arrival, people started listening to the preachers who called on everyone to repent.

They set their slaves free, forgave debts, began treating each other with exceptional kindness, began taking care of the poor, the widows and the orphans. People shared their riches and opened their hearts to the strangers in their midst. They made peace with enemies and they forgave the mistakes of their friends. It was a time of extraordinary generosity.

And then the appointed hour came and passed. Nothing happened. And so, the people gradually went back to their old ways.

However, something *had* happened. The messiah had come in the form of love, equality and kindness. But no one noticed.

Messianic consciousness lives within us as a seed of infinite potential. *Moshiach is coming* when we are awake to her seed within us, when we notice the miracle in our midst. All we can do is water that kernel with our keen attention, honor its truth, and surrender to the possibilities that God reveals as our journey unfolds.

Planet Burger

There have been moments of my life of journeying when I have been stopped dead in my tracks by debilitating depression. My normal sense of life as a wondrous journey has at times been interrupted by periods of confusion and paralysis. At times like these, I have felt like the ancient people of Israel: immobilized, enslaved in Egypt before they had the strength or even the awareness to cry out.

At one such time I was living in the hills above Berkeley, California where the beauty of the expansive view from my house contrasted cruelly with my contracted and depressed inner state. The combination of chronic physical pain brought on by a car accident and the devastating emotional pain of a crumbling marriage sent me under the covers, unable to move from my bed.

As I lay there quietly searching for the strength to get out of bed, I heard a voice whose tone was quite insistent. "Go have a Planet Burger!" it said. Now, I don't often hear voices, and this message was so clear, so firm, so adamant. The only place I knew that served Planet Burgers was a restaurant down in Berkeley called The Good Earth.

I immediately got up, got dressed and drove there. Miraculously, I found a parking space right in front, and as I walked up to the door, the restaurant was just opening. I was led to a booth in the corner of the room and I promptly ordered my Planet Burger and some Good Earth Tea. As I waited, I was filled with a sense of expectancy, even hope.

The vegetarian burger was indeed delicious. Halfway through my meal, four large, well-dressed African-American women came into the restaurant and were seated in the very next booth. The whole place was empty, and I had been enjoying the quiet. Why did they have to be sitting in the next booth? Immediately they erupted into loud, enthusiastic conversation, and I had no choice but to listen.

"Sometimes," drawled the first woman, "You just gotta leave Egypt!"

"That's right," the next woman replied, "Sometimes, you just gotta leave Egypt." And then the other two joined in, saying, "Yep, it's true... sometimes you just gotta leave Egypt!"

I sat there dazed, too stunned to even hear the rest of their conversation. I finished my Planet Burger, drove home, stepped into my house, gazed out the window at that expansive view of the bay, and knew for certain that my journey was guided and blessed.

In the Native American practice of vision quest, you choose a place in the wilderness, delineate its borders, and then sit there for some period of time—a day, three days, a week. It is a time of fasting, prayer, and being attentive and receptive to the message, blessing, and challenge of *The Great Spirit*. That small space that you have consecrated becomes a microcosm of the whole world. In this consecrated space you sit and watch for signs.

In truth, the signs are always there. But we must be in a receptive and humbled state to receive those signs. When I'm on a vision quest, I pay attention to the ant that is crawling from east to west carrying a large crumb. I notice the cloud above my head dissolving into mist. I listen carefully to the call of a crow and discern the scent of rain in the breeze that blows against my face. Suddenly the whole world is crowded with messengers, and my task is to become still enough, open enough, to receive the *word of God* disguised as this world.

Once I was leading a day-long retreat at a beautiful house in the suburbs of Philadelphia. The retreat culminated in a solo practice that was one hour long, called *Hitbodedut*, which is similar to a vision quest. We each found our spot at the edges of the yard and sat there to pray and become receptive. About 45 minutes into my practice a car pulled up near where I was sitting, and a man addressed me. He yelled from the car, "Do you live here?" I pulled myself out of my reverie and tried to respond… but I couldn't find the words. I was just dumbstruck with the profundity of his question. He repeated it a couple time, "Do you live here? Do you live here?"

When I didn't respond he just drove away in a huff. And I sat with that question and it expanded within me as a challenge. How might I fully inhabit this incarnation, this family, this tribe? How might I fully inhabit this glorious and sometimes troublesome body that I have been so generously given? How might I take responsibility for the care of my body, my family, my community, and this amazing planet? Do I live here?

Later, of course, I realized that the man in the car was lost and was just looking for someone to give him directions.

But for me, he was a divine messenger who had come to challenge me and invite me into a deeper level of acceptance and integration.

At home, I tend to fall into routines and I sometimes get complacent. Traveling helps me to wake up, heighten the skills of my attention and open myself to messengers everywhere.

Seeing

When I was 14, I quite suddenly developed a fascination with the idea of going to Israel. I wanted to ask God a question that none of my teachers had a good answer for, and I had a feeling that the Holy Land could absorb my question and take me closer to my own truth. I wanted to walk on the land of my ancestors and step outside my small life into the larger mythic realm of holiness.

My parents balked at the idea, mainly because they didn't have the money to finance this trip. The more they tried to talk me out of it, the more obsessed I became. I called all the rabbis in my county and asked them to contribute money for my trip from their discretionary funds. I found a program that was a camp during the week and then placed kids in Israeli homes each weekend.

As I begged and cajoled, there was one particular argument that my parents put forth that got under my skin. They said I was too young to appreciate what I would be seeing. I was absolutely determined to prove them wrong.

When finally, miraculously, I was on my way, I made a vow to open my eyes as wide as possible, to see fully and clearly the amazing sights I would be privileged to behold. I vowed not to miss a moment of it.

My determination to prove that my parents were wrong about me opened a door into a state of extraordinary presence. Each day, I was transfixed by the light, by the colors, by the beauty of the land and the diverse array of people from across the wide world who were drawn there.

One day we visited Akko, an ancient city in the northern Galilee that was built on steep cliffs at the edge of the Mediterranean Sea. We toured a Crusader era fort that had been converted to a jail. Climbing the steep stone steps, I felt transported into another world. I peered through the gap between massive stone and looked down at the street below. Instead of the cars and commerce that were supposed to be there, I saw winding cobblestone passageways crowded with donkeys and what looked like people of the distant past, buying and selling their wares. I stared for a good five minutes at this impossible sight. It was as if the veil that separated me from the past had lifted, and I was *there*. I could smell the market and feel the dust rising and hear the shouts of the people and the brays of the donkeys. Just as suddenly as the scene had appeared, it vanished. And I was staring down at the cars and trucks of a modern town.

I was enchanted. Later that evening I shared with my roommate what I had seen. She just nodded awkwardly and reported me to the head of the camp.

The next day I was called into his office. He motioned me to sit down and with a tone of kindness and concern, asked me what had happened. After I described my experience and told him what I saw, his alarm was quite evident.

He leaned toward me and said, "You imagined this."

And I said, "I saw it!"

In a tone even more serious, he repeated. "You imagined this."

And at first, I protested. "No, I really saw it."

A moment of silence passed between us and I realized that if I didn't "admit" that I had imagined the whole thing, the camp director would have to send me home. And so, I reluctantly conceded, and learned a sad lesson. For many years I was afraid to share my visions, intuitions, dreams or perceptions, except through poetry or song.

I still tap into that determination not to miss anything, and that amazing quality of expanded presence that allows me to see beyond the narrow confines of our culturally agreed-upon Reality.

Seeing becomes a meditation, when I open to color, light, shadow, texture, shape and form… all the while letting go of thoughts, definitions and associations that arise. If I look at a tree and immediately say "Oak," I run the risk of dismissing that creature that is rooted before me, and missing that particular and essential being who has her own voice and place and spirit.

If, on the other hand, I can notice that it is an oak, but set aside my label, admitting the enormity of what I don't yet know… then there's a possibility of really meeting that amazing being and receiving her gifts.

For me the pinnacle of travel is stepping into this unknown, this mystery of otherness. That majestic branch sweeping toward the sky, those gnarly roots grasping the Earth, and the light shining through this leaf illuminates an intricate hidden world of green.

To see, I need to slow down, follow the arc of my curiosity. And follow the sparks of my intuition. My intuition tells me that the infinite is hiding inside this finite realm, and if I am determined and willing, that treasure can be unlocked and revealed.

My Elemental Journey

The subtitle of Rob Brezsny's book, *Pronoia*, is *How the Whole World is Conspiring to Shower You with Blessings*. It represents a shift in perception, whereby we open to God's Presence in each and every moment, and suddenly all the everyday, though hidden, miracles become obvious. God comes to us disguised as this world and it's our job to become receptive and responsive to this shower of blessing; it's our job to unmask the world so that we might know our very experience of each moment as the play of God that surrounds and infuses our lives. We do this work by opening up our senses and our hearts, by becoming acutely aware and keenly curious about...absolutely everything. The Koshnitzer Maggid, a spiritual master who lived in the eighteenth century in Poland, had something to say about this *Everything*:

"Everything that exists is composed of the four elements," he said, in his book *Avodat Yisra'el*, "fire, wind, water, and earth. And these elements are in opposition to one another. For example, water extinguishes fire, while wind fans its flames. Each of the elements exists in a complex relationship with the others. This claim that such diverse and even oppositional elements can come together and form compound matter defies all logic. But they do. A spiritual force unites them and completes them...and that is God."

I look into the world and let the forces of Earth, Water, Fire and Air awaken the awareness of each of those elements within me.

With the element of **Earth,** I open to a sense of belonging and connection. I become fully embodied, nurtured and nurturing. I feel my stability and resilience. I learn how to compost the mistakes of the past, and I celebrate every phase of growth from sprouting through flowering all the way to decay. I feel myself connected to every phase of the cycle of life renewing itself. I become reliable, trustworthy and rock-steady. My roots reach down into the core of this planet, grounding me in love, connecting me to my lineage.

With the element of **Water,** I learn to flow. I can finally access the full force of emotion, creativity and intuition. In the depth of my water element I reclaim the ability to give and receive love and affection. I become expressive, empathic and generous. I connect myself to the Source of all flow. I am washed clean of impurities.

With the element of **Fire,** I find my passion. I learn to focus my attention and assert my will. With Fire, I explore my power to create and destroy. I learn about energy. I cultivate the full force of my enthusiasm, idealism, drive and sense of purpose, while tempering all that energy with humor and joy. I work at transforming fire into the kind of light that will heal and illuminate, burning away every resistance to God.

With the element of **Air**, I open to the wide expanse. I cultivate curiosity and break open the confining structures of personality and conditioning. I expand into the far reaches of imagination, and I open to new perspectives. With Air, my thinking is clarified and information is organized. I become spacious. I can watch the workings of the mind with detachment, witnessing thoughts come and go like the changing weather.

When I find these elements within me, I look out and notice that the whole world is indeed conspiring to shower me with blessings. With this new awareness I can open to receive those blessings.

The Cheerios Miracle

Traveling as a spiritual practice requires a certain suspension of disbelief. I need to open my mind and expand the range of what I deem normal or even possible. Only then will I see the miracle that was always there waiting to be revealed.

There have been special moments in my life that challenge my conceptions of Reality and send me to a place of wonder. In that wonder-place I put down my compulsion to figure it all out, and just enjoy the thrill of mind-blowing miracle.

One such special moment happened to me in church.

I was living in upstate New York, doing odd jobs, playing guitar and singing in a band. One of my part-time jobs was as a sexton in an Episcopal church in New Jersey. A couple times a week, I drove down and cleaned the church from top to bottom.

One early Sunday morning I woke up and had just enough time to grab a cup of tea, jump in the car, and race down to New Jersey. For some reason I couldn't understand, I woke up thinking about Cheerios. This was strange because I hadn't had a bowl of Cheerios since I was a kid. During the whole 45-minute drive to Jersey, all I could think of was Cheerios, and I resolved to go to the store and buy a box as soon as I finished cleaning the church.

As I mopped and dusted, I'm thinking, "Cheerios, Cheerios." Taking out the trash, "Cheerios, Cheerios."

Cleaning the windows, "Cheerios, Cheerios."

Then I came to the sanctuary, and as I polished the pews, I still couldn't get the idea of that breakfast cereal out of my head. The last thing I did at the church was vacuum the rich red carpet of the sanctuary. I slowly pushed the vacuum cleaner down the wide center aisle, thinking, "Cheerios, Cheerios," and there at the end of the aisle, right in front of the altar, standing out against the rich red carpet... was one... single... Cheerio!

I stopped, quickly turned off the vacuum cleaner, bent down, picked up that Cheerio and popped it into my mouth. I savored its familiar shape and taste. I gloried in that timeless moment, feeling whole, and holy, and completely satisfied.

I believe that we all experience moments of miracle, but when we can't find a place for them in our Reality maps, those moments just slip away as if they never happened. If we can't find a reasonable explanation for that bizarre happening, we might just blot out the memory of it. We spend our lives constructing a worldview and fortifying the rigid parameters of what we all agree to be Reality.

When something happens that definitely doesn't fit into those parameters, either that something must be dismissed, or our worldview gets blown up and the boundaries of our conceptions of Reality crumble.

Those happenings like the Cheerio Miracle Moment

might send me on a path of building a new conception of what's Real, but that's not where I wanted to go. It was enough to be left in a state of profound suspicion. When I remember and celebrate those moments, I am reminded to always suspect that whatever Reality map my mind invents is probably only a miniscule fraction of the larger Reality I have only glimpsed. Knowing that I don't know the whole of it is the beginning of wisdom. Knowing that I don't know sets me on the path of love and adventure.

Another moment: Traveling through Deland, a small college town in the northern scrublands of Florida, I met a group of spiritual journeyers who came together once a week to do "astral travel." The leader had a large presence and a gentle voice; the members of this group seemed calm and kind, so I joined them.

At our first meeting, we sat in a circle, closed our eyes, and the leader guided us into a deep meditation. I've always been told that I had a good imagination, so I followed the leader's instruction easily. He led us to an elevator and told us to enter, push a button and let the elevator take us to exactly where we needed to go. When I stepped out of the elevator, I was suddenly flying, and I spent the whole time of my journey flying over a vast ocean. After some time, the leader asked us to come back to the elevator and return to the place where we had begun.

I opened my eyes, and the woman who was sitting next to me turned toward me and said, "Oh, I saw you flying over the water."

In that startling moment, my mind just stopped. The

tone of her voice was so matter-of-fact, so casual. I didn't respond or react; I just nodded and smiled politely. But inside! Inside, my world had just been turned upside down. My whole life—of separating what I imagined inside me from the objective reality outside of me—was suddenly thrown into an endless sea of doubt. I mean, if someone else could see me doing something I thought I was merely imagining... perhaps imagination was not what I thought it was. That recognition was the beginning of a cascade of realizations. I was cracked open, and knew that I'd never be the same.

That's what travel can do, if we dare to step off the ledge of what we think we know, into the seeming abyss of miracle.

The Lessons of the River

"I would love to live like a river flows, carried by the surprise of its own unfolding."
—John O'Donohue

My river story starts many years ago. I was a shy 22, making my way across the country. I met up with some folks who invited me to join them for three weeks in the wilderness of Utah. We floated down the Green River and hiked deep into majestic canyons. Far from civilization I found my strength, my wild beauty, my fierce commitment, and a deep unselfconscious joy. The wilderness gave me the seeds of wisdom that germinated slowly over years of effort and grace. The river filled me with a momentum toward a life of adventure and exploration.

Flash forward many years later: I was leading a pilgrimage to the Grand Canyon. We spent just one day floating on the Colorado River. I leaned back in my boat and heard a voice rising from those cold waters. "I have a message from the Green River," the voice said, "She wants you to come back." I was startled, but immediately I said, "Yes."

When I arrived home, there was a message on my answering machine from Eli, who was a river guide and a rabbinical student. "Would you like to lead a journey with me down the Green River in Utah?" I called back and said, "Yes, definitely, yes."

We put the word out, set the date for the following summer, and called our journey, "A River flows from Eden" (a quote from Genesis). Slowly people began signing up.

Then toward the end of November, I was awakened in the middle of the night by another voice; the voice identified itself as the Green River. She said, "Here is the curriculum. This is what I will teach you." I jumped out of bed and wrote down the words.

Flow... Connection to Source ... Constancy/Change ... Purification ... Generosity/Receptivity ... Buoyancy/Trust ... Depth.

The following summer, we set out from Moab, for the deep sundrenched mysterious canyons. We stepped into our canoes and opened to the wisdom of the river. As pilgrims, we knew that the beauty and grandeur of the outer landscape mirrored the vast inner landscape of soul. And as we floated down Labyrinth Canyon, the wisdom of the river began to emerge.

Flow: I learn to pay attention to what obstructs the flow. What gets in the way of the flow of Life? Shame? Self-consciousness? Rigid desperate ambition? Attachment to preferences? My fixation on the *drama* of my story? When I bring my attention to the graceful dance of flow, I see how each moment opens the door to the mystery of what's next. I live my life in a state of surprise. I am swept up in the currents of inspiration. I let go. I am embraced by the current, conveyed into my potential.

Connection to Source: The river shows me that I am connected to the source of all life through my gratefulness, through my receptivity, through my openness. That Source-place is within me, overflowing. The river tells me that I must connect with Source within, heal the places of disconnection, connect again and again. Then I can be a channel of inspiration, strength, love and wisdom.

Constancy/Change: Everything in my life changes; everyone dies; all I see is flux, and I am flummoxed. The river knows this well, changing constantly; and yet, it is only the forms that change. There is essence beyond these shifting forms that speaks to me, that whispers its constancy. There is an enduring spirit that calls to me, and I listen, so that I might gracefully endure the changes that ripple through my fragile life.

Purification: The river calls me to self-awareness. When I discover the obstacle to flow—when I uncover the true nature of my resistance to becoming one with the river—it is possible to transform my insight into an offering. I give my awareness to the water's purifying power. I offer up my self-imposed limitations to the Divine force of flow that it might wash me clean. Toward the end of our week together, we look around the circle and someone says, "We're all getting dirtier on the outside and cleaner on the inside."

Generosity/Receptivity: As the river keeps on giving itself, I keep opening to receive its nourishment. The place of fearful stinginess in my heart is cracked wide open to reveal my own true generosity. That generosity is expressed through my simple joyful presence, through my loving attention.

Buoyancy/Trust: The river teaches me to float, to be carried forward. The river shows me how to say *Yes* to every obstacle, to trust the onward motion of my life. Just for an instant, I stop flailing, and all of Life supports me. In surrender, I am empowered.

Depth: As I paddle my canoe, I am continually searching for the calm surface that reveals the depths. I am looking for those same depths within me, which will manifest as a calm, radiant and beneficent surface. The person who is *deep* embodies the wisdom of the river: Flow... Connection to Source ... Constancy/Change ... Purification ... Generosity/Receptivity ... Buoyancy/Trust.

Driving home from this incredibly rich experience, I realized how important it was for my sanity and inspiration to spend time as a pilgrim in the wilderness. First, I thanked the Great Mystery who guides me and then I said, "When can I do this again?"

The answer came a couple years later, during a conference where I was teaching about the power of Earth, Water, Fire and Air. On the day of Water, I woke up to a very large, fierce Presence in my room who identified herself as the Amazon. "I am the Mother of all rivers," she roared. "You must come."

I was a bit shaken by this encounter, but I pulled myself together and thoroughly enjoyed teaching about the power of water. At the end of class, a young man from Brazil came up to me and said, "Would you like to lead a trip to the Amazon?" I just laughed out loud and blurted out, "Oh my God, I just manifested you!"

He connected me with the other people at the conference who were from Brazil and we planned a full, rich exciting trip to Brazil that included workshops in Sao Paolo,

Rio de Janeiro, culminating in a five-day pilgrimage to The Great River Herself.

When the Amazon invited me, there was no way I could refuse. To embark on a pilgrimage is to step into the unknown and say *yes* with every step.

Journey to the Amazon

After teaching workshops and leading services for the Jewish communities of Sao Paulo and Rio de Janeiro, I set out for the Amazon with four other brave souls to lead a pilgrimage to the greatest river on earth—a place of incredible fecundity and diversity. There we encountered a wide array of birds, monkeys, and fish. We swam with pink river dolphins and marveled at wild orchids. I went there to honor a sacred place that is so crucial to the health of our planet. I went there to express my gratefulness for the blessing of abundance, biodiversity and lush beauty. We explored the Rio Negro, which is the largest tributary of the Amazon and has the great distinction of being nearly mosquito-free. Apparently, the mosquitoes don't like the river's dark tannic waters, which was fine with me. Every day on the river was a new adventure. My pilgrimage coincided with the high-water season when the forests are flooded. In small boats we could search deep into the jungle to discover its secrets. All week it felt as if the mother of all rivers was giving us her beauty and revealing her mysteries.

On our last night of the journey, the eco-lodge where we were staying was offering a moonlight boat ride to learn about caimans, amazing alligator-like creatures that sometimes live for 75 years and may grow to a length of 18 feet. At first, I didn't want to join the tour because I knew that the guide would catch a caiman for us to pet and it didn't feel exactly right. But I wanted to be on the water in the moonlight, so I decided to go.

The guide indeed caught a young caiman, about two feet long, and held it captive while poking and prodding and teaching us interesting facts about her anatomy. This caiman was a small young one with an ancient face, and I sat there horrified; not that he was hurting her, but still it felt awful. I felt like I was inside that caiman being poked and prodded. And I felt ashamed.

In the middle of the night I woke up filled with remorse for being part of this. I went to the river to ask for forgiveness. I spoke to the spirit of the caiman too. It felt like this demonstration had been about turning Nature into an *"IT"*, an object for our entertainment, amusement and curiosity. The whole purpose of my pilgrimage was to address the river and all her creatures as a *"THOU,"* to encounter each being with a reverent awareness of her own inherent majesty and worth. After I cried and expressed my remorse, a giant caiman swam by and lifted his nose out of the dark waters, as if accepting my apology.

The sunrise signaled that it was time to begin my return journey home. I carried home with me all the blessings of the river, along with a fierce determination to protect these sacred waters from our attitudes of arrogance, from our habits of plunder and exploitation.

A Way that is a Flow that is a Call

Mother of All Rivers,
Mother of All,
Mother.
The whole world suckles at your breast.
Sacred flow, four thousand miles from mountain to sea,
Removing the silt of our dying past, quenching the
    undying thirst of this entire planet,
Teeming with a vast array of untamed life, color,
    fragrance, mystery.
You have called me.
A sloth staring solemn and sweet, her three toes clasping
    at anyone
who will listen.
You have called me.
A golden monkey chattering in her ancient tongue
matching the cadence of our chant.
You have called me.
At the Meeting of the Waters, love and awe mingle in my
    heart.
In the night a caiman lurks with eyes shining,
and Anaconda stretches out beneath our boat,
Unseen dangers call me to attention, to aliveness,
to remembrance.
A pink river dolphin's smooth joyful weight against my
    hand,
her flippers wild and strong sweep past my legs.
Beneath these dark waters, shiny pink flashes of light

calling to me.

Our boat glides through quiet jungle, past egret and
orchid

and then meets the storm of a wide rough expanse with
waves that mimic the sea,

The sea—that's where we're all going,

And it is the way there that is holy.

A way that is a flow that is a call...

Come home.

Go and Bring Blessing

Hitchhiking through Italy, I was picked up by a young German man who lived with his parents in a small village outside of Cologne. He gave me his address and invited me to come visit. About a month later, I took him up on this offer and boarded a night train to Germany. I remember that night well, because it was very dark and foggy, and this was the first time I would set foot in Germany.

My grandparents came to America from Hungary and Lithuania. Their families that had been left behind were murdered by the Nazis. My uncle died fighting the Nazis. My father survived his battles with them. Though we rarely talked about this when I was growing up, I noticed that my parents would never buy something if it had been made in Germany. In those days, no Jew would be seen driving a Volkswagen.

On that gloomy night I stared out the window of the train which slowed to a halt as we crossed the border into Germany. All I saw was mist rising through barbed wire. A German official in uniform was moving through the train checking everyone's passports against a crumpled list he carried.

I was so scared, I could barely breathe.

My visit to Germany turned out to be fine. I pushed that fear down inside me, as I tried to look long and hard into the faces of the old people I met who had lived through the war. Everyone was polite. No one wanted to talk about what had happened.

Many years later when I received an invitation to teach in Berlin, I felt that buried fear rise up and show its face. Berlin wasn't just Germany. In my mind it was a center of death, destruction and doom.

When I prayed and asked for guidance, I received a very clear message: "Go and bring blessing."

When I heard and absorbed this message, all my fear was suddenly gone—replaced by a sense of purpose and a sacred mission. I purchased my ticket and had the intuition to extend my stay an extra day.

All through my visit to Berlin, I remembered that my purpose was to bring blessing. I felt extremely useful. My sacred mission filled me, inspired me, humbled me and gave me such strength for my journey. There was absolutely no room for fear, and no possibility of being a victim.

And that extra day in Berlin just happened to be November 9th, which was the 20th anniversary of the toppling of the Berlin Wall *and* the 69th anniversary of Kristallnacht, the violent day that marked the beginning of state-sanctioned terror against the Jews of Germany and Austria.

During the day I joined in a grand and joyous celebration of Freedom, and at night I marched by candlelight in commemoration of those whose lives and hopes had been shattered. In the crowd that night were dozens of police in uniform, participating as part of the march and rally. I was so moved by the sight of their shining faces and I spoke with one of them. In broken English he explained that they were off-duty but wanted to wear their uniforms to make a statement of caring and solidarity with the victims of Germany's dark past.

I had come to Germany to bring blessing, and left feeling that I had been blessed.

My rule of travel is twofold: Bring blessing wherever you go, and receive the blessing of the place.

To bring blessing, I simply open up and allow the Divine flow of goodness to pour through me toward each being or place I encounter. To accomplish this, I must first let go of judgment. That's the hard part because I am fairly attached to my judgments.

If I'm sitting in an airport waiting for my flight, I can bide the time by watching the people around me. If I am judging, then I'll notice who I like or have an affinity for and who looks creepy to me; who seems mean or depressed or angry; who seems friendly or nice; who dresses well; and who looks rumpled and tired. I can watch the interactions of people with children and judge their parenting skills. I can watch how lovers treat each other, and muse about their relationship problems. All this can be very interesting, but the downside is that when I am judging, I become a victim of other people's moods and energy, and I begin objectifying the world around me. When I judge, I often begin comparing myself to others. Whether I feel better or worse than that person sitting near me doesn't even matter; in both instances I have separated myself.

In contrast, I can take the stance of blessing. I can allow

the Divine flow of goodness to pour through me toward each being or place I encounter. This takes people watching to a new level. With each person I notice, I can explore the possibility of wishing them well.

I really don't know if it makes any difference to them, but this flow of blessing certainly changes me. With each wish of goodness, compassion, kindness or peace, I can feel the quality of my own presence shift and expand. While judgment separates me, blessing connects me—not just to the recipient of my blessing, but to the flow of goodness itself.

Blessing in secret this way feels so delightfully subversive, and I like that.

I enjoy this practice so much in fact, that I almost always request a window seat on the plane. I like to sit by the window for a couple reasons. One: I always want to be aware of the miracle that I'm *flying*! And two: I can look out and send blessing down on the land far below me. I imagine some unsuspecting stranger walking out to her car and suddenly getting hit by the flow of blessing pouring down from the sky. She looks up briefly, startled by the smile spreading across her face for no apparent reason. And I'm up there, looking down at this peopled planet, smiling, too.

Ancestral Healing

At the first touch, I knew I'd be taking a journey. Robert, a healer at the Villa Sumaya on Lake Atitlan in Guatemala touched me in a way that made me know I would be safe and accompanied on a journey of truth, the truth that was locked away in my body. The body doesn't lie, but sometimes it waits for the right moment to be heard. That moment had come.

There was this spot in the middle of my back, about half way down and little bit to the right of my spine, that was always a tad tender. It was just how I was built, and it didn't bother me much. The strange thing was, I once was massaging my mother's back, and she had the exact same spot, and when I mentioned this to my sister, she also had the exact same spot on her back—tender, ticklish, sensitive to touch.

As Robert explored that spot on my back, I found myself swept into a vision. Under a steel gray sky my great-grandmother turned and was shot in the back, murdered by the Nazis as she stood outside her village in Hungary. Watching this tragedy unfold, at that same moment, that spot in my back released and my tears began to flow with the grief of generations, finally unbound.

The next step came just a couple weeks after returning from Guatemala. I had signed up for a workshop with Rabbi Tirzah Firestone on "Healing Ancestral Trauma." As I sat in a circle of rabbis and Jewish Spiritual Directors, I knew that I was ready for this work, this opening, this healing.

Some background: When my mother's father, Emre, came to this country from Hungary, he became Elmer. He completely divorced himself from the past, from the *old country*, from the devastation of Europe. I experienced his presence as a veritable edict, barring the whole family from ever looking back. We were Americans now, and the past was not worth our attention. It was gone. The woman he married, however, loved all things Hungarian. Bertha, my grandmother, held fast to her connection to her past, to the food and blessing of her birthplace. My grandparents had left their parents behind in Hungary. As the plight of the Jews there deteriorated, the letters stopped coming. I can only imagine the grief and guilt that sent Elmer forward, and Bertha back.

Bertha died in Cleveland just three days after I was born in New York City. My mother's doctor convinced my father that he must lie to my mom about her mother's death, so that she could stay safe in the hospital with me. My father said he had to go to Washington, D.C. on a business trip. When he got back from Bertha's funeral, he had to tell my mother that her mother had died of a stroke and that she was already buried. My mother was understandably furious. I don't know if she ever forgave him. With two young children and a newborn, there weren't many opportunities to grieve. I was told that I cried nonstop for three years, perhaps crying the tears that my mother couldn't afford.

As I sat in the circle at Reb Tirzah's workshop, I knew it was time to reconnect with my lineage, to open to the blessings of my ancestors. "I am willing," I said to Tirzah, to my colleagues and to the endless line of ancestors who were waiting for my heart to open to their blessing.

During the workshop I opened the channel of communication and blessing with my great-grandmother, whose wound I had carried all these years. She witnessed my life and radiated joy across the generations. She delighted in my accomplishments. She also reframed the time of my birth as a cause for celebration. "When you were born," she said, "I was reunited with my beloved daughter Bertha."

From my great-grandmother's perspective, the story of my birth was transformed from one of tragic betrayal to a story of love and celebration.

Just a few months later, I completed the journey by traveling to Hungary with my sister and cousins to touch the *Motherland*, the home of my ancestors.

The moment that I stepped on to the land, a circuit was completed, and I felt a charge of pure joy. The current flowed into me and through me, and I became the grateful conduit between past and future.

Flora and Fauna Teachers and Friends

When I come to a new place, I want to befriend the unique plants and animals of that place. They are my guides, my teachers, my companions who hold the wisdom, and exude the fragrance of *this* particular place. They have adapted in order to survive and thrive over countless years. They have information that I need. They can help me unlock the hidden beauty and wild spirit that can only be found *here*.

When I spend time with the ancient Bristlecone Pines that grow gnarly and crooked above 12,000 feet high in the Sierras, they whisper their secrets on the high winds—when I am patient and still enough to listen.

When I come in the spirit of reverence, honor and curiosity, I always feel some response from the plant and animal kingdoms.

I went on a pilgrimage to find a giant Kauri tree in New Zealand, down a secret trail known only to the locals. Kauri forests are the most ancient in the world, but their numbers have been whittled down by extensive logging. This particular tree was kept secret for its protection. The Maoris revere the Kauri as King of the Forest. I heard that there is a saying repeated whenever a great person dies that translates as "The Kauri has fallen in the sacred forest of Tāne."

When my friends and I found this royal tree, we circled its trunk and sang songs of honor that floated up to its tallest branches which formed the canopy for a large patch of forest.

When I arrive in San Diego, I like to stroll around and marvel at the gardens of succulents whose fantastic shapes and textures inspire my whimsy. It's no wonder Dr. Seuss lived near here.

In the Sonora Desert, I am stirred by the almost human shapes of Saguaro Cacti; in the cloud forest of Ecuador, I am awakened by wild orchids and a vast variety of hummingbirds.

In the backwaters of Florida's Cedar Key, I paddle into a raft of white pelicans who quite casually accept me as one of the flock. Their welcome reminds me that I am home, and possibly that I am always home.

Are We There Yet

I led a pilgrimage to the Galapagos; the theme was "Learning Praise from the Animals." On these remote islands, the animals had not been conditioned to fear humans, and so our encounters with them were frequent and friendly. What I was teaching I was also learning myself: it is possible to praise our Creator just by wholly inhabiting the fullness of our own nature; just by shining the light that we are; just by being ourselves, with unselfconscious awareness and enthusiasm for Life.

The climax of my Galapagos adventure was the opportunity to swim with the sea lions. We hiked across Floreana Island to their secret cove and jumped into the clear swirling tide. The sea lions immediately surrounded us, excited to play. All afternoon we frolicked in delighted abandon with these sweet and bold teachers of the sea. When I got back on the boat I was inspired to sing this line from Psalm 34:13: "Who is the one with a passion for life, loving every day, seeing the good?"

I imagined that through their play, the sea lions were asking me this very question. And I answered without hesitation, "I will be that one. I promise."

I travel to explore my passion for life; I travel to express my love for each day; and I travel to look for the good. The flora and fauna are my guides on this path of passion, love and seeking.

Here I Am!

In the Wilderness, I encounter the naked truth. When I walk into that wilderness I leave behind the defenses and protections of my possessions, conceptions and self-definitions. There, in the wilderness, it is possible that I will open to a message that I can no longer avoid or deny. Perhaps that message has been there, within me, all along. Suddenly, in the wilderness, the whole world is speaking, reflecting back that hidden message and opening me to the naked truth of my life.

I had a friend who lived at the edge of a vast mountain forest and I asked him if I might use his home as the starting point for my 24-hour vision quest. I left early in the morning, carrying nothing but a blanket. I walked up into the mountains searching for my spot. My vision quest practice is to find a place in the wilderness, delineate its boundaries (about ten feet square), and then sit there in prayer. That sacred ground becomes a microcosm of the whole universe and a reflection of my inner state.

I walked for about an hour and chose my spot along a ridge overlooking a lovely mountain stream. I couldn't actually see the stream, which was obscured by Ponderosa Pines, delicate aspen shoots and a tangle of scrub oak, but I could hear its music. I listened all day and all night to the sound of that stream. Its music became the soundtrack for my inner drama, washing me clean of boredom, fanciful stories, difficult self-judgments. Its music kept me awake to the hidden beauty that flowed through my own dark night as I shivered and pulled my blanket around me like a womb.

When the morning finally dawned, I felt wide awake, buzzing with the life of the forest. I decided to end my quest by dipping in the stream that had been my joyful companion through the long cold night. I climbed down through the brush, took off my clothes and gloried in the cool life-giving waters. By then the sun was shining its slanted rays through the trees so I sat in the tall grass that lined my river, to breathe in the morning and dry off.

My reverie was disturbed by a sound coming from across the meadow. I peeked out from my riverside nook, only to see a very large black bear rubbing its hindquarters against a tall Ponderosa Pine. He was completely absorbed in the pleasure of that scratchy tree, making little rough sounds of delight.

I watched in utter amazement, hardly breathing, transfixed by the sight of this magnificent creature who had blessed my quest. I was filled with awe and gratefulness, and I watched that bear for a few minutes in absolute reverence.

Then, in a moment everything changed. That bear lifted his head and began lumbering toward the stream behind me, and was completely oblivious to my presence. I was crouched in the grass between a very large bear and his bath.

Immediately my mind went into overdrive and time seemed to slow down. It felt like I was quickly consulting an encyclopedia in my brain flipping through the chapters saying, "Bear-bear-bear-bear-bear..." till I came across an entry that read, "Get really big and let the bear know you are there. You don't want a startled bear to trip over you on the way to his bath."

The bear was just 20 feet from me and closing in fast. I jumped up, spread my arms wide and in a very large and deliberate voice, shouted, "HERE I AM!"

The bear immediately stopped in his tracks and casually trotted off to the side to find his own place at the stream. I heard a splash and then he was gone.

My heart was beating wildly and all I could hear was my own voice reverberating within me. HERE I AM! The message was clear. Be as big as you really are. Let the world know that you are there. Hiding is dangerous. Pretending to be small is not an option.

Our ancestors journeyed into the wilderness to encounter the naked truth.

In the Torah, as God calls to each of them by name, they each answer with the word, "*Hinayni*" which means "Here I am."

And that is our journey as well. Each of us is called. Each of us is called out of hiding. We are each called to expand to our true breadth, and claim our place, and grace this world with the fullness of our presence.

The Path of Love

In December of 1987 I was riding in the backseat of a car in Gainesville, Florida. Having just dropped off the sound system for my concert, we were going back to rest before the performance that evening. I remember leaning forward, sticking my head between the front seats to say something to the two guys in front. I remember exactly what I said. "My birthday (which was not till April) is going to be on Shabbat this year!"

We were stopped in the left lane, behind someone who was waiting to turn. Dennis, who was driving, ignored my enthusiastic, seemingly irrelevant proclamation. He looked in the rearview mirror and calmly said, "He's not stopping."

A large vehicle was barreling down on us, and in the next second, crashed into the back of our car. This all seemed to happen in slow motion. Because I had been leaning forward, I ended up jumbled between the front seats, arms and legs tangled up in a suddenly much smaller car. The back seat was gone, crushed by what turned out to be an Entenmann's Bakery Truck.

The driver of the truck rushed over and asked, "Is everyone alright?" I had the presence of mind to say, "No." When the emergency vehicles arrived they needed to use the *Jaws of Life* to pry open the car so we could be extracted from it. While they worked, something very strange happened.

The only way I can describe it is that the car filled up

with love. There I was, mangled in a crushed car with some seriously broken bones and who knows what else … and a pink golden light was pouring into the car, saturating the space, cushioning its hard edges, softening my heart, and opening a sense of absolute wonder.

As I calmly surveyed the scene of devastation and destruction, I remember saying to myself, "This … is love?"

During the year following the accident, as my whole life fell apart, I kept that question in my heart as a *koan*, a riddle. That question became the context for the physical pain of my broken body as it healed, for my emotional pain as my marriage imploded, and for my spiritual pain as the momentum of the life path I had been on came to a screeching halt. "This is love?" I asked again and again. The answer was always, inexplicably, *Yes*.

The rug had been pulled out from under me, and I was falling. I was falling. I was falling. And strange as it may seem, I was falling in love.

This love was different than anything I had ever known before. It wasn't warm and fuzzy. There was no particular object for this love. It was a force that transcended pleasure or pain. It was a force that was so big, so powerful, and I was in a place of such brokenness. All I could do was surrender. The more I surrendered, the more I could feel myself held in an embrace that was as wide as the universe. And then in spite of all the pain, my heart expanded and filled up with a delicious longing.

My outer situation had not changed. I was still in dreadful pain, in a terrible marriage, and had almost no money or support. And yet my inner situation had radically changed. I was deeply, impossibly in love. And I knew that my life would need to be an expression of that intoxicating love.

That love took the form of wanting to serve. My service became my calling, and my calling took the form of spiritual leadership. My leadership eventually took the form of becoming a rabbi. I wasn't in love with Judaism or with any form or creed.

I was in love with God.

Leaving everything that I knew—my marriage, my home, my community—I packed only what could fit into my car. I stepped onto the Path of Love with perfect faith that Love was calling me, sending me and guiding me.

Whenever I get too distracted from that core calling to express my love for God through this world, I suffer terribly; and nothing makes sense. When I again return to the Path of Love, I feel connected, sustained and invigorated.

Shortly after my husband Rachmiel and I fell in love, he said to me, "I'm so glad that you love God more than you love me." He could feel that my love for God was a deep pool, a resource from which all my love flowed. He also knew that my relationship with God meant that I wouldn't be expecting anything from him that only the Divine could give me.

Jewish liturgy refers to the Great Love (*Ahavah Raba*). The prayer says, "With such a great love you have loved us." When Rachmiel and I came together we each realized how flawed our own puny, limited, conditional love really was. We knew that what was called love could be so mixed with selfishness, lust, greed or shame, that it might do as much harm as good. And so, we decided to aspire to a different kind of love.

In our marriage vows we each promised, "I open to The Great Love that it might pour through me to you."

Stepping on to the path of Love means getting out of our own way, to let the Great Love flow. It means trusting that Divine force and offering ourselves as willing channels.

The path of Love is the most rigorous spiritual path there is, because when I make a commitment to that path, I am making a commitment to clear every obstacle to the flow of love through me; I am making a commitment to the work of dealing with my own resistances, moment to moment. My resistance is made of the defenses I have built to protect myself. Yet those same defenses have kept me imprisoned in the illusion of separation.

The Path of Love leads me step by step, back into connection with the truth of my heart, and with all of Creation.

Coincidence

They say that coincidence is God's way of staying anonymous; well, I say she's not doing a very good job. All that effort to stay anonymous fails in the light of certain moments of incomprehensible happenstance. And one day you realize that your whole life is made up of these moments. You shake your head and say, "What are the odds!" But it's not really a question because you know that the odds are impossible to compute. And then you go back to living your life; what else can you do. But your mind is irrevocably *blown*. When this happens often enough, it chips away at our shared Reality map, and you begin to wonder about such fixed constructs as Time, Space and Identity. In the light of certain moments of coincidence, the old paradigms that tell you time moves in just one direction or that each place has a fixed location, or the self has discrete boundaries—it all begins to blur and fade and then we are left floating in a void that inspires both terror and the spark of infinite potential.

That's when God shows her face.

Rachmiel and I decided to spend six weeks at the beach. We needed to come down from the mountain and stare into the waves. We needed to surrender to our own inner currents. I was experiencing a time of endings, grievings and unknowns. Instead of trying to immediately jump in to what's next, I knew that it was time to just *be*, to deepen my inner practice, slow myself down and wait for the signs that might guide me forward.

We found the perfect cottage on the beach. The fact that it was Mission Beach was not lost on me. Yes, here was a place where I might attune to my "mission" and how to fulfill my soul's purpose, to look deeply, with spacious discernment. Our place was one of the original wooden cottages still standing after all the other ones were torn down to make room for more upscale and modern vacation rentals. We could sit on the couch and look out through the river of passers-by on the boardwalk to the sand and sea beyond. We watched the ocean change moods and tides. We watched for dolphins doing their joy-dance across the waves, flocks of pelicans soaring in formation, and surfers ever patiently sitting and waiting for just that wave.

I was slowing down, stabilizing my attention, harnessing my awareness, finding my stillness so that the muses can find me and speak.

And then I got an email from John, an old friend from college who I hadn't seen or spoken to in 40 years. He wanted to let me know that a mutual friend was critically ill; John included his phone number with a note that said, "Feel free to call me." So I called him. We talked and began catching up about our friend and then about 40 years of wandering through our respective wildernesses. When I mentioned that I was in San Diego, John's voice sweetened as he told me that in 1984 he spent a very important and pivotal time there, in a little yellow shack on the beach at the corner of Seagirt and the Boardwalk in Mission Beach. "That's where my life was saved," he said.

"Wait!" I yelled. "I'm in that house right now." I emailed

John a picture and he said, "This seems too impossible; in the first place this cottage of yours is *exactly* the same shade of yellow as it was in '84; secondly, neither the roof nor Dutch door show any sign of having been so much as spray-washed in the last 34 years—this tiny shack, 3,000 miles from where I sit. This shack you're staying in is where my life was saved."

It was a moment of miracle. After suddenly becoming deathly ill, John was diagnosed with a rare autoimmune disease. His only hope was to move to San Diego and participate in a drug trial. "The drug had no taste," John said. "I knew that they had given me the placebo." As John settled in to the little yellow shack, he met and fell in love with the woman who lived next door. "Love healed me," John said.

Then 34 years later I move into that very same place, where love has healed, where miracles reverberate. I tell John that this time in my life is about stepping into the void. And John remembers, "My time in Mission Beach in '84 was, by far, the most significant 'step into the void' that I'd taken by that time in my life."

John and I scratch our heads and pause in wonder. Finally, I say, "I'm thinking that this miracle is a sign that I am in the right place, that I should look to love as my healer, that I should know that the Great Choreographer is guiding this dance in ways that I could not imagine."

Walking

For millions of years our human ancestors were on the move. We followed the migrations of the wild, hunting for sustenance. We followed the seasons of growth, gathering the herbs that might heal and nurture. Always moving on, called by a rhythm of life unfurling through season and migration, like flocks of birds listening to an inner wisdom of timing and navigation, touching down to perch gently, yet ever listening for the call to move. That ancient rhythm is still in us. How could it be otherwise?

Our settled life came only after millions of years of knowing this rhythm, this dance of grace and wisdom. Our settled life is only a tiny fraction of the heritage of being human, a thin veneer, yet it has smothered and obscured that ancient treasure almost completely. And though our settled life has bequeathed to us the many wonderful gifts of civilization—agriculture, security, science, and technology, to name a few—those gifts have come at a price.

In my traveling life, I have had moments of touching that ancient treasure, feeling its light shining out from deep inside my DNA, giving me just a glimpse.

I was feeling the shadow of mortality, about to turn 60, when the call to travel hit me hard. It was to be my *proving-to-myself-that-I-was-still-alive* journey. I went to a website that touted the "10 Most Beautiful Hikes in the

World," and was immediately enchanted by the look, feel and aura of the Queen Charlotte Track, on the north coast of the south island of New Zealand. I had once tried to set up a teaching gig in New Zealand through a friend who lived there. "They are not ready for you yet," my friend had explained. I called her again. "I think that New Zealand is ready for you now!" she exclaimed, and then helped me set up a few gigs that could pay for my trip.

I asked one of the graduates of my training if she might be my traveling companion. Judy was a great chanter, with a sunny disposition, loved that part of the world, and though she was older than me, Judy was a bit more fit and was my inspiration. I wanted a journey that would be challenging, but not too difficult. We found that perfect balance in glamping (a blend of glamour and camping). Our glamping journey on the Queen Charlotte Track allowed us to walk all day along a magnificent and rugged trail on the spine of a ridge that passes through lush coastal forests with breathtaking views of the Queen Charlotte and Kenepuru Sounds. At the end of each day, we found our luggage waiting for us at a simple yet elegant cabin. After a hot shower, a glass of superb local wine and a delicious meal, we fell fast asleep and were raring to get back on the track the next morning. My old knees were so grateful to be walking with a light load instead of a heavy pack.

Judy and I chanted as we walked, *Va'asuli mikdash v'shachanti b'tocham*—Make for me a Holy Place so that I can dwell within you. The sanctuary we are commanded to build in the Book of Exodus is portable. In fact, the whole story of Exodus and our journey to the Promised Land hearkens back to an earlier and primal nomadic wisdom. Connecting to that wisdom is crucial to our freedom. Those 40 years in the wilderness represent the journey we all must take that will reconnect us with the ancient rhythms that are buried inside us.

Think of it: The Sanctuary (in Hebrew, the *Mishkan*—literally, the dwelling place of the Divine) is portable. We are commanded to build that Divine sanctuary with all of our generosity and artistry. It is meant to express our complex beauty and over-the-top elaborate and extravagant imaginings and yet—it is portable. It's as if God is saying, "Make for me a place within you that is of ultimate beauty, but don't get bogged down; don't let the complications and bulk of your endeavors weigh you down or slow you down or keep you from the essential lightness necessary for the journey."

As I walked the Queen Charlotte Track, I began to feel that lightness and the ancient rhythm within me. So, on the fifth day, even after all the challenges and effort of hiking, I didn't want to arrive at any destination. I knew that the Promised Land was within me. And it was the movement, the dance of my journey, that fulfilled that promise. I just wanted the hike to be my life.

Sometimes when I am walking, and I forget for a moment that I have someplace to go, I can feel the earth turning beneath my feet, and the sky opens wide. There is a buoyancy to my step and my senses sharpen. The ancestors who still live within me are stirring, moving me onward.

Paying Homage

My father loved bridges, so on our family vacations we traveled to see every kind of bridge: beam bridges, truss bridges, cantilever bridges, arch bridges, tied arch bridges, suspension bridges, cable-stayed bridges, double-decked bridges, covered bridges. Each one filled him with awe and reverence.

When my father died, I built him a bridge that spanned a narrow arroyo on my land in New Mexico. The bridge has a plaque that says, "The Leon J. Katz Memorial Bridge," and a bench that leans against the tallest Ponderosa Pine. I sit on that bench and lean back into the fragrance of butterscotch sap, thinking of my Dad and his quiet reverence for bridges.

It wasn't enough to love bridges, learn about them and admire them from afar. From my Dad I learned that you must go and pay homage to what you love.

The dictionary tells me two definitions of that word homage. Originally to "pay homage" was to engage in a "feudal ceremony in which a person pledges loyalty to a lord and becomes a vassal." In the ceremony, you would put both your hands between the hands of the lord, giving yourself to the obligations of vassalage, while receiving the gifts of safety and sustenance.

The other definition is anything that "shows respect or attests to the worth and influence of another."

I pay homage in order to acknowledge the gifts I have been given. This act of tribute actually allows me to integrate those gifts more fully, and weave them into the fabric of my being. Saying thank you for "the worth and influence of another" completes a circle in a way that makes me feel more whole.

When I was 16, I became a vegetarian at a time when this was considered very weird. All my mother's friends told her I was going to die for lack of protein. I wandered for a few years trying figure out a diet that was healthy, delicious and morally conscious. Then I discovered the Moosewood vegetarian cookbooks, and I was suddenly connected to an instant community who were living out the best of my hippie dreams, merging compassionate politics, whimsical aesthetics, and creative cooking. I followed every recipe and then learned to improvise, anchored in the principles that the Moosewood collective espoused at its restaurant in Ithaca, New York.

So, when I had the opportunity of finally stepping inside the hallowed halls of the Moosewood restaurant, it felt like there should be a feudal ceremony. I would have liked to have heard trumpets. I wanted to place my hands between the gloves of Lord Moosewood, and bow down in obeisance.

Everyone there was too busy to notice that I was having a religious experience, paying homage to the Mecca of a food movement that had educated and nourished me. Even though no one noticed, it was important for me to go there, eat lunch, say thank you, and honor the worth and influence of the visionaries who had helped to shape my life.

Sometimes we must journey great distances of space to honor a place that has influenced us. And sometimes we need to travel just as far through time.

My time-travel journey was inspired by an invitation to teach in Columbus, Ohio. I jumped at the opportunity. My parents met and courted each other at Ohio State, in Columbus. I wanted to go there and honor their young love. I had heard the story of how my father got sick and missed their first date, but brought a dozen yellow roses the next time and won my mother's heart. Every year there were yellow roses on our family's kitchen table.

My mother and father are both long dead, and my memories of them are marred by illnesses, both mental and physical. I wanted to meet them before they were encumbered by the complications of raising four eccentric children, before struggles set in and set up patterns of stress and conflict. Somehow, I knew that if I went to the place where they had met, I would be given a glimpse of that *before*.

When I arrived at the campus, I asked around to learn what was the same as it was back in the 40s. I learned that the only place that definitely hadn't changed was The Oval, a wide-open green, crisscrossed by dozens of pathways.

So, I stood in the very center of that Oval and opened my heart. I came to stillness at the center of all the bustle. I rooted myself there and found a sense of deep silence within me. Then I opened the eyes of my heart and saw The Oval in about 1943, students all around me, rushing to class, dressed in the fashions of the day, yelling to each other, joking, jostling, filled with youthful enthusiasm. I watched for a while till I spotted my parents. They looked so very young, so hopeful. They were laughing as they swept by me like a rush of Spring wind. It just took my breath away to see them so beautiful, so carefree.

I stood there in The Oval to pay homage to their love, their optimism, their adventure—which would invite me in and form the doorway for my miraculous life.

At the Crossroads

I have set before you Life and Death, blessing and curse.
Choose Life!
—(Deuteronomy 30:19)

Not just once a year, once a week or even each day, but
every single moment and with every step, we can choose
Life. This means choosing to let go of a negative thought
or judgment; choosing to live with uncertainty; choosing
the kind word or generous attitude; choosing to let go of
tension and relax. In every moment we can choose to be
chosen by God for the best possible life, for the life we were
meant to live fully. In each moment, we can choose to accept the gifts, challenges, opportunities and responsibili-
ties that we are being given.

This spiritual challenge of choosing Life can only be
taken up when we learn how to *stand before God*—which
is religious language for coming into full awareness. In
standing fully before God, we can finally embrace our
whole selves completely. We can take responsibility for our
choices.

I was once asked to lead High Holy Day services at a
large Mindfulness retreat that was to be taught by Thich
Nhat Hanh, a Vietnamese Buddhist teacher whose reputa-
tion for gentleness and wisdom drew hundreds of follow-

ers. The retreat was scheduled during the Jewish Holidays, and the organizers thought there might be some Jews at the retreat who would benefit from the presence of a rabbi. In preparing for the retreat, I wrote to Thich Nhat Hanh to explain what we'd be doing at his gathering and I sent him a few books about Judaism so that he'd have a better understanding of the importance that these days held for his Jewish students.

At the opening session, he welcomed the Jews who would be celebrating their holy days at the retreat. In a tone that was both incisive and tender he said, "It is my understanding that the purpose of all Jewish practice is to live every moment in the awareness of God's Presence... and that is Mindfulness."

He understood that to stand in God's presence means to stand outside the whirlwinds of change, anchored in the stillness of center, shining out the fullness of our own presence, attentive to the truth of this moment. From that still center, from that open-hearted awareness, the choice between Life and Death, Blessing and Curse at last becomes clear. Until we can stand before God in a state of calm, alert clarity, all the layers of distraction, turbulence and conditioning will rob from us the freedom of choice. And so, as we rise to the challenge of choosing Life, we must learn to stand before God, or as Thich Nhat Hanh explained, "to live every moment in the awareness of God's Presence."

We're already in the presence of God. What's absent is awareness. And awareness is the essential factor that allows us to choose life. The kind of awareness I'm talking about has two components. As I journey, I am distinctly aware of this very step, this breath, this miraculous moment; while at the same time, I cultivate an awareness of the whole journey—the long winding road that led me here and the great mysterious possibilities stretching out before me.

Shortly before he died, Oliver Sacks, neurologist and best-selling author, described the view from where he stood on the precipice, at the crossroads between a life well lived and the great unknown.

He said, "Over the last few days, I have been able to see my life as from a great altitude, as a sort of landscape, and with a deepening sense of connection of all its parts."

Through my own meditation practice I am beginning to see that it is only by entering fully into this miraculous moment, this breath, this step of the journey, that I'm able to achieve the "great altitude" that will give me a perspective on the landscape of my life, a perspective that will reveal that undeniable "connection of all its parts." Entering this moment means letting go of distraction, releasing my worries about the future and regrets about the past, letting go of the surface of life so that I can receive the depths.

Underneath all of our conditioning, habit, prejudice, neurosis, complacency and numbness, we can find that core something that is true, essential, and uniquely authentic. We might call it your soul... or your God-self. At our core we are unconditional Joy, unqualified Love. And there, we are profoundly connected to each other. We are simply One, and living inside the Unity.

So, we journey to strip away all those extraneous layers. We journey to circumcise the heart, cutting away the obstacles to love in all its fullness. Our journey challenges us to release all of our defenses and dissolve all our stinginess born of fear, and finally give ourselves away.

The crossroads of choice is the moment when prayer happens. Though prayer seems like a lot of words, in the end, prayer is not about saying words, singing songs, or thinking deep thoughts. Prayer is a stance, an attitude toward Reality. It's a way of living this moment in the awareness of God's Presence, addressing ourselves wholly to this mystery... while at the same time cultivating the wider view, the "great altitude." I think we come together in prayer to support each other and give each other the courage to take this stance. It's so easy to lose our awareness, to fall away from the "great altitude," and fall prey to the tyranny of emotions, the addiction to self-image, and the false promises and seductions of this world.

The Christian mystic, Richard Rohr, teaches that it's no accident that the first of the Ten Commandments is the one that says *I am YHVH your God who brings you out of constriction, out of slavery.* It's first because if you don't have "one God before you," you will either become your own god or make something else into a god. And when you do that, you are back in constriction, back in slavery.

Choosing means being able to sometimes stand against the flow of mainstream culture, and to stand for values that are positively counter-cultural... values like introspection, kindness, slowing down, inner calm, acceptance of differences, humility and faith.

Faith is the choice that we make to live with uncertainty, to live with paradox, to resist cynicism. Having faith doesn't mean that we think some God-in-the-sky will intervene. Faith is an end in itself. In Faith we plumb the depths of our humanity to find our Divinity. In Faith we lift ourselves up into the "great altitude," to glimpse the mystery of connection within our own landscape and between all of us.

Eric Hoffer the street philosopher said, "In times of great change (which is always), learners inherit the earth, while the learned find themselves beautifully equipped for a world that no longer exists." Faith itself is actually a stance that allows us to be learners, continually growing, learning from our mistakes and loving the questions. From that fragile stance of Faith, we are free to keep choosing Life in these times of great change, because from my stance of Faith, I can imagine what is possible and even what might seem impossible.

Each moment we are standing at the crossroads, between Life and Death, between Blessing and Curse. And sometimes the only reason we choose Life and Blessing is that we start down a road that we've been down before, and we remember that it's a dead end.

All of our travels have brought us to this moment of great change. The world that we thought we knew no longer exists. We are always standing at the crossroads, the place of choice. We are always being called to awaken to the blessing before us, to Life.

The Unending Journey

The foundational story of Judaism, which is remembered, celebrated and relived every single day, is a story of a journey. In the Beginning we journey into existence. Then we journey with Abraham into the unknown and then into the entanglements of family dramas. We journey from there down into Egypt (which in Hebrew is *Mitzrayim* and means "the narrow place") and into the suffering and constriction of slavery. Our journey from slavery to freedom, from Egypt to the Promised Land represents the journey of awakening.

Major Jewish holidays celebrate important points on that journey. On Passover, we commemorate the leave-taking; on Shavuot, we celebrate the Receiving of Torah at Mount Sinai along the way; Sukkot reminds us of both our fragility and abundance as we journey forth.

In fact, everything that is important to our spiritual development as a people happens *along the way.*

There is a yearly cycle of readings from Torah that all Jews follow, which leads us from the very beginning of Creation to the moment when we are about to arrive in the Promised Land. And then we never really get there! After all that anticipation, all that promise... we start over again... we're right back at the beginning.

If the destination was the point of it all, then this might become very frustrating. *But it is the journey that matters.*

We read this story again and again, discussing, analyzing, and extrapolating on it endlessly, because it is meant to be a mirror for our own soul's journey. By reflecting on our journey, we are meant to wake up to both the wonder and magnitude of each and every step, and the amazing miracle of the whole journey in all its glory, absurdity and sweetness.

There is a way that these two awakenings—to the miracle of the journey and to this step right here beneath my foot—are symbiotic awakenings. The moment when I can step back and marvel at the twists and turns, synchronicities and blessings that have brought me to this here and now… is the moment when I realize that this step matters. And when I walk with that awareness, deliberately opening to the Grace of each step—then I receive a vision of the wide perspective of my whole amazing life journey.

Sometimes I look around and see each and every one of us walking the path of the valiant hero on a remarkable journey, filled with the human adventures of birth, illness, romance, divorce, loss, triumph, heartbreak, healing and aging into wisdom. And yet we often just accept it all as boringly normal and tedious.

I travel to remember that my whole life is an extraordinary adventure. I travel to awaken my curiosity and wonder, so that I can bring those qualities to every step of Life. When I am awake in this way, I am living a paradox: With this step, I have arrived in the Promised Land; all there is to do is celebrate. And I'm also forever on my way there, stumbling, dancing, opening to all it means to be human—remembering that it is the journey that matters.

About the Author

Rabbi Shefa Gold is a leader in Aleph: Alliance for Jewish Renewal. She received her ordination both from the Reconstructionist Rabbinical College and from Rabbi Zalman Schachter-Shalomi. She is the director of C-DEEP: Center for Devotional, Energy and Ecstatic Practice.

Shefa composes and performs spiritual music, has produced ten albums, and her liturgies have been published in several new prayer-books. She leads sacred journeys and teaches workshops and retreats around the world. Named "One of the 33 most Inspiring Rabbis in America," by the Jewish Forward, she combines her grounding in Judaism with a background in Buddhist, Christian, Islamic, and Native American spiritual traditions to make her uniquely qualified as a spiritual bridge celebrating the shared path of devotion. She is the author of *Torah Journeys: The Inner Path to the Promised Land*, and *In the Fever of Love: An Illumination of the Song of Songs* published by Ben Yehuda Press, and *The Magic of Hebrew Chant: Healing the Spirit, Transforming the Mind, Deepening Love*, published by Jewish Lights. Shefa lives with her beloved husband Rachmiel in the mountains of northern New Mexico.

For information about Shefa's teaching schedule, visit her website: www.rabbishefagold.com

Are We There Yet